Midnight to Morning

Jacqueline Tsui

BookLeaf Publishing

Presentation by *BookLeaf Publishing*

Web: www.bookleafpub.com

E-mail: info@bookleafpub.com

ISBN: 9789395969932

First edition 2022

DEDICATION

I would like to thank my friends and family as I've learned so much and share many wonderful and meaningful experiences with them. Some of them directly inspired my writing in this book. Thank you to Book Leaf Publishing as well for challenging me to write this collection.

PREFACE

Most of the poems are based on or heavily inspired by my own experiences. A few are purely creative ventures. Nevertheless, I hope you enjoy reading them, and that it inspires you to write about your own experiences, or simply write for fun!

Midnight Stories

On sleepless nights, in quiet spaces
There is no relief for my racing thoughts
Entangled like a thousand laces
My heart is distraught

Many sleepless nights I have had
Sometimes spontaneous visits
Bringing me tears I don't understand
and troubling memories in snippets

I have many questions in life
Most of them are unanswered
So on these sleepless nights
I let my mind wander

I write songs and letters
and trouble myself over
whether I could have had better
On the search for closure

So on these sleepless nights
I speak to those around me
While their minds are in twilight
I tell my midnight stories

If I Had a House

There
Is a kitchen
spacious enough to walk around in
There is a garden big enough to plant flowers and
attract ladybugs
There is a room big enough to sleep two people
There are windows big enough to let sunlight in
There is a dining table where we can eat together
There is a couch where we can sit down and talk
There is space for joy, sadness, frustration, anxiety
Relief, nostalgia more and everything in between
There is space for the burdens and pain we carried
As well as space to welcome new hopes and dreams
If I had a house, it would be big enough for us to
Share our happiness and troubles, and all the little
things in between
Hold my hand, let us take the first step together, into
our new home

A Little Bird Asked Me to Go on a Walk

I've been going to the promenade in the evenings
A little bird suggested ten-thousand steps every day
It is helping me with my sleep quality
Even though it is not the easiest thing to do
The weather in Hong Kong has been decent lately
At the very least, the sun is visible
I really should put on some sunscreen
Before I go out for my daily walks
Nevertheless, I made a promise to myself
And to the little bird who cares about me
I put on my worn grey shoes and head downstairs
Where the sea is only three minutes away
Let me tell you, ten thousand steps takes at least
An hour and fifteen minutes to complete
And that is if you brisk walk, not stroll

There are many people at the promenade
People from all walks of life walking the same path
Even the sun is walking at the same time
It is a moment of separate togetherness
Some are faster than me, some are slower
Some are immobile, sitting on benches
We are thinking different thoughts
Feeling different things
Some of us have already had dinner
Some are about to head home

But we are all watching the same thing

The descent of a fiery glowing orb beyond the mountainscape
And how beautiful this moment in time is
I cannot see others' minds
But I can tell you what I am thinking
I wish my little bird were here with me

The Lost Summer

I lost the summer
Even when I held her in my hands
She could have stayed forever
For her I would build all my plans

Her leaves were thick and warm
But they fell away before I could reach them
Scattered by rain and storm
A few of the branches were bent

I chased the sun that set everyday
I cast my line in aquamarine
I followed the trail of fish travelling from the bay
And yet, I still lost her

I lost the summer
When my heart found the river bottom
A lark hung it on the needle of fir
To pass me onto autumn

I chased the sun that set everyday
I cast my line in aquamarine
I followed the trail of fish travelling from the bay
And yet, I still lost her

Pink and Blue

A streak of pink cloud follows closely behind
The tail of an aeroplane shooting through the blue
The echoes of the rumbling engine
Linger in the sky like remnants of a story
Wonder where it's heading? Wonder who is piloting?
Perhaps someday I'll meet this person
And collect another tale
Pink and blue
Opposite yet complimentary
An enigmatic combination
Of human and earth
We see the planet, the planet sees us
Beauty lies within all
The rumbling fades, soon it is silent, but not for long
As the song of birds refill this space

Boo

One day a door opened
A gust of wind brushed past
She saw a blue figure frozen
A poorly decorated mass

And so she laughed

He found it annoying at first
Picked her up and moved her aside
All she had to do was reverse
Tumble into his arms eyes wide

And so he fell in love

Sulley and Boo
He showed her the world anew
Travelled through doors in two
The captain to her crew

One day Sully opened the door
He looked back one last time
Then closed it, seen nevermore
Her pursuit would last a lifetime

Sully and Boo
Fell apart like her ponytail
Life's rite of passages brew
Captain Boo ready to set sail

Over land and on water
Boo travelled far and thorough
She opened door after door
Closed every single one too

Sully and Boo
She would remember him forever
Wiser because of what she's been through
But no more happier

I still think about you
But I don't know who you are
You cut the string between us loose
And we have drifted too far

But the show must go on
I will become the woman you couldn't see
When day breaks above days bygone
I will step into the sunlight alone and free

Omphalos

Train tracks run beside the park where I used to play
for hours
Signaling the passage of time as they rumble by
The lovely aroma of the coffee shop in the university
Welcomes me as I turn my back on the orange sky

As I imagine myself walking along the garden path
back home
I can almost hear barking and other household noises
And as I enter the big wooden front door sweaty and
tired
I can almost feel loving hands and hear gentle voices

Sometimes I wonder why I never returned
When it's only a 45-minute train-ride away
I'm reminded of my hectic life
No time for reminiscing every day

I decide to return once and for all
And as I make my way to the front door
I see the muddy footprints of a stranger
The doormat no longer looked worn and torn

A place out of reach, yet so near I can't miss it
I take the 45-minute train-ride back home
back to the present, real-time, reality

Evelyn

Parts of you were ushered in
Lovingly by the waves in blue
She sees again the boat named Evelyn
And feels her hope renew

Disorganised pitter-patters leave footprints
Sand-covered hands scoop up the shells
Put close to the ear and listen for hints
It is where your heartbeat dwells

Roof of the cabin kissed by the sun
Hands tight around her knees
Flowing dress, hair in a bun
She wishes for the day to never cease

Ocean brings little bits of you
Closer and closer to her
From a small collection of few
To being filled with mementos of you

The house, her home, where she awaits
The shells, to listen to your heartbeat
The rusty pocket watch for asking fate
'Is today the day he claims this empty seat'

The pearl necklace for her wedding
The jar with the blank note and unwritten words
It delivers, gentle and caring,
Love songs sung by little birds

Strands of silver hair succumb to the wind's
beckoning
The blank note is still unwritten
She sings her last song beautifully
Heartbroken but still utterly smitten

With an invisible angel, a cloud in the shape of you
who whispers her name with the passing boat
The note where sweet nothings are laid onto
Is what has always helped her float

But now rain pours as she drifts away
Tears from heaven for her unrequited love
The boat that happens to come every day
With her name embedded above

The jar pushed into the sea by a curious little one
The pearl necklace from an ungrateful teen
The pocket watch of a deceased son
And she, never again to be seen

Parts of you are ushered out
Back into the ocean, scattered like art
The boat Evelyn still sails the sea
Oblivious to breaking her heart

Ha-na

Yellow are the sunflowers
Overjoyed with your adorableness
Ultramarine are the bluebonnets
Amazed at your courage
Red are the roses
Enamoured with your loving nature
Sapphire are the forget-me-nots
Opened by your willingness to respect
Brown are the columbines
Emboldened by your fortitude
Apricot are the Nikko day lilies
United with you in your challenges
Teal are the Hydrangea
Illuminated by your beauty
Forest green are the Bells of Ireland
Unconditional in their hopes for you
Listen closely, how much they are saying!

I Think There was Something You Wanted to Say

When you were cradling a newborn me in your arms
When I climbed into your embrace to escape storms
When you saw stock prices rise
When you bought your first queen-size
When the woman was touching your thigh
When you stayed out late to avoid explaining why
When you were bellowing and howling your dissatisfaction
When you used the house's deafening silence as a distraction
When you were weeping like a tortured dog
When you were lying limp in the pervasive fog
I heard your gut-wrenching sobs
I heard your ear splitting complaints
I never knew what you wanted to say
Even when you yelled until your voice strained
You once brought us a cheap McDonald's meal
With kid-sized fries and burgers
You tore open the packaging for ease
With your large stubby fingers
Mom would be furious if she were there
But it made two eight-year-olds' day
It was one of the only moments
I understood what you wanted to say

Who are you?

I'll start with some fireworks
A whole feast planned
In disbelief at the universe
Who delivered you to my hands

Who are you? I don't know yet
But I know you are stunning
I'll wrap you up in your little duvet
No I'm never running

I'll be yours, and you'll be here
Here with me
I'll give you my best, my dear
Be set free

We'll drink from the loving cup
Work hard to make it happen
You'll be here, growing up
Painting the world with your talent

I promised myself I won't have you
Until I have guarantee
Maybe one day I'll get to meet you
And take you to the sea

Who are you? Are your eyes as brown as mine?
Who are you? Is your heart as strong as mine?

I'll be yours, and you'll be here
Here with me
I'll give you my best, my dear
Be set free

Celia

Running, running at a wicked speed
From the jaws of sincere greed
She fell down a rabbit hole, as Alice does
And sunk into a bed of pristine dust

She held her hand up, a damsel in distress
A gesture too much like a jest
Dust infiltrated, penetrated, bit at her lungs
Not another breath to see a final song sung

Eyes closed, breath slowed
The smell of grass being mowed
Gentle fingers around one's neck
The caress of breezy happiness on the deck

Disappeared like the condiments set out
Paws on her stomach, to her face a little snout
'Time's up', said the little man
She did not want to live again.

Through a Sheet of Ice

The world through a sheet of ice
No matter how thick or thin
Gloveless hands upon it does entice
And pricks like a glimmering metal pin

A blue, blue world
And a shivering, breathless one too
Not very nice for bee-stopping curls
Nor faded glasses recalling who's who

But a necessity to be pricked
As cold hands wrap around one's neck
One knows not to be tricked
By a silly peck

For the touch of a Primrose
Tempted by the budding Petunia
Blinded by childish eros
And entangled in minutia

For the joining of hands, painting of faces
Suffocating laughter and bundled backs against each other
You pick, weave, and tear apart the laces
Like an abandoned infant crawling for another

The sunlight blinds you, it sears into your eyes
Look away and you shall see the blue
All nightly ventures are beautifully constructed lies
And your grievances a ready-made stew

Endless lusting after fossils, you fall into
Footprints of a long-deceased offence
And soil bakes you a distinctive blue
Annihilation becomes not preference but defence

Incessant lust, an disgusting red hue
But merely a house of cards
Look away and you shall see the blue
And find nothing to safeguard

If I Could

My eyes are a thousand kilograms heavy
Stretching my lids to the earth's core
My head is swaying back and forth
Like a broken bottle washed ashore

My fingers are outstretched and immobile
As if reaching for an invisible object
My legs are collapsed, knees on the floor
Like the fate that was sealed and set

A lifetime's fatigue condensed in a quarter
A thousand arguments immortalised in a little brain
I wore my heart on my sleeve at the beginning of life
Now I lie unmoving in the pouring rain

Once, I dreamed of wild sunsets
And seeing them with my loved ones
But we talk with our backs against each other
Trying to undo what cannot be undone

Once, I dreamed of the sweetest cake
And how that sweetness would fill up my heart
But it has been emptied of its contents
And scattered in parts

I would spend my hours
Smelling grass under warm sun rays
Trying to find flowers for the little girl
Would occupy my whole day

This is what I would do
For the little girl who wore her heart on a sleeve
But who would do all this
For the woman lying in the withered leaves?

New Mother

Over the moon, under the sea
From wandering albatrosses, to deepwater squid
All embarked on their journey inland this eve
Led by a new mother's bid
Her song spread so far and wide
Her joy epidemic-like
"Look!" she excitedly cried
Eventfully marked by fate's chime
A circle of only three
A whole universe in embrace
How incredible it was to be
Loved so infinitely in the human race
Till the ends of the earth
She would sacrifice her all
Nothing short of a miracle was his birth
Her whole world was so small!
The squid laid gentle eyes on them
A little boy just took his first breath
The albatross sang for them
Bliss filled the deepest depths
Where her tender fingers are
His little hands rest above
Nothing else matters
Endless is her love

Thank You, Honey

You took both of my hands in yours
Over a cup of hot chocolate with cream
You listened to the pain in my heart
Until my tears evaporated with the steam

We went our separate ways in a few hours
And moved onto our own errands
The heat from the cup, warmth from your eyes
Lingering like sun-burnt, summer sand

My life may be falling apart
My soul may be losing its way
But oh will I still smile
Every time I think about today

My Black Hole

It's got eyes blue as ice
Tail sharp as knives
Claws big as planets
It'll take what it can get

I try not to swim close
But that lasts a couple weeks at most
Like a moth to a flame
The game of life bends to pain

Why can't you see it, I ask
They said it's an impossible task
undetected by the lucky heart
Invisible to the untrained eye

I have a black hole
It's feeding on all of me tonight
It's a never-ending battle
To salvage what's left of me for the light

Do you feel it too?
Sorry, I'd rather not turn you blue
But it's irresistible, this demand
of holding onto your hand

Why can't you see it, I ask
They said it's an impossible task
undetected by the lucky heart
Invisible to the untrained eye

I have a black hole
It's feeding on all of me tonight
It's a never-ending battle
To salvage what's left of me for the light

There's a whole world out there
of pleasure and pain to bear
That's the price of the journey
The price of being alive, being able to see

I can see it, I say
It's black and blue and grey
It's a never-ending battle
But I will never settle
I'll push and struggle and keep breathing
Until I come free with new wings

I’ve Got the Blues

Teal
the almost-morning sky
Clothed in my powerpuff girls pyjamas
I peeked through my room window
The ground where I picked fallen berries
was grey turning white

Indigo
my various denim jeans
ranging from small to large
over the years
i’ve dropped and gained the pounds

Turquoise
the waters where the sea meets land
on the sandy beaches of Cyprus
where my little bird and I
dipped our weary feet

Admiral
the tote bag I bring everywhere
when I don’t have to carry a lot
nor travel too far
from where I live
where my family is waiting

Before No More

Follow up on that hotpot meal
before the restaurant
goes out of business

Take that diving qualification
before work
engulfs you in itself

Go on that camping trip with friends
before their faces
cement in faded photos

Say 'I love you'
before your loved one
leaves this earth

Say 'I miss you'
before the person you miss
believes your silence

Say 'I am sorry'
before things
become irreparable

Lead your own fate
Despite your past
Take your own hand
Even when someone is holding it

One life
Infinite beginnings
Step by step, day by day
Start now, start anywhere
Before everything becomes no more

To My Best Friend

We fought vacuum cleaners and toolboxes
With their terrifying long arms and orifices
We survived an Angler fish attack
And a harrowing elephant sacrifice

You braved the wasp colonies with me
While my anxiety was through the roof
You endured disgusting larvae clusters
While I panickingly steered our canoe

You rode the waves of life with me
Despite my tendency to submerge
Like a quiet submarine chugging along
Making sure I re-emerged

We rode frogs and spiders
Traversing an infected garden
We flew on golden eagles' backs
Reversed time for tasks forgotten

We returned turtle hatchlings to their mother
Stopping only to have snowball fights
We collided two gigantic moles
During our frantic, exhilarating flight

You were my brain when I was overwhelmed
by the hustle and bustle of living
You were my climbing buddy
Hand in hand below mountains awaiting

We went ice-skating, DJ-ed, and played chess
In between space journeys and heaven volleyball
We saw ethereal planets and bioluminescence
Turned into limes and body-slammed flowers so tall

You let me whack you endlessly
and win chess in mini-games
We raved at the little people's nightclub
and sightsaw on a colourful toy train

All the dreams we talked about
I still hold dear to my heart
The little things we enjoy in life,
No matter how little, can still be told apart

Thank you for being there for me
Despite being a thousand miles away
Although the game has long ended
I hope you will always choose to stay

What Lies Ahead

I had a dream that
I descended into the living room
On a cold lonely midnight
Full of desperation and gloom

The little girl was in her pyjamas
Face in her hands that dripped salt
It looked like she was at her wit's end
And believed her life had come to a halt

I waded through the heavy air
Heavy as her desire to resign
I kneeled down in front of her
And cupped her hands in mine

Oblivious to my presence
'Darling,' I said, looking up
Almost unbearable to listen to
Her quiet sobs and hiccups

'I am here with you,' I said
While I caressed her hair
It was thick and lush, soft to the touch
Not entirely lost to the storm's wear and tear

'I am so proud of you,' I cried
'You will get through this,' I affirmed
As I embraced her in my ghostly arms
And reality beckoned my return

I am sliding across stage
Upright, tall and proud
My hair is long and wavy
Adorned by my beautiful gown

A thousand smiles hang in the air
But all I think about is the rat race
That I've finally broken free of
And troubled me for the last two decades

I have a ticket to the new world
I no longer have to mould my life
Around textbooks and exams
At the end of the tunnel was, afterall, a light

I go back home in the morning
But the light blinds me, I cannot see clearly
I wait for the dream to arrive
and the woman who holds me most dearly

To tell me not what lies ahead
But that it will be okay
That she is so proud of me
That in time, I will find my way

www.ingramcontent.com/pod-product-compliance
Lightning Source LLC
Chambersburg PA
CBHW051750130826
49812CB00033B/1091
9789395969932